BASIC TRAINING

How to Prepare for Your Spiritual Quest

ASHLEY PORTER

Allow your light to shine. God has amazing things in store. Don't give up.

Ashley

purposely created
PUBLISHING

BASIC TRAINING
Copyright © 2015 Ashley Porter

Published by: Purposely Created Publishing Group™
Author photo taken by: Delisa C Photography and Design

Printed in the United States of America

ISBN-10: 1-942-83821-2
ISBN-13: 978-1-942-83821-0
Women's Version

DEDICATION

This book is dedicated to YOU!

If you have a pulse, you have a purpose.
No matter what anyone says, thinks, or feels
put God first and allow him to use you.

The moment we submit and say, "Yes," is the
moment our real life truly begins.

Thank you and God bless you.

TABLE OF CONTENTS

OPENING PRAYER

"The Lord is near to all who call on him, to all who call on him in truth." Psalms 145:18 (ESV)

Lord, I pray that every person reading this book hears from you. I pray that they activate their faith and place all their trust in you, Father. Strengthen each person with wisdom to understand your word, discernment to do your work, and courage to live out loud for you. I pray that the spirit of fear and confusion be canceled right now. Those whispers of "I can't" be transformed into a strong "I can." Lord, comfort those who are hurting; help them to come to you with their pain, help them to know that you are the ultimate healer.

Lord, you are awesome and we thank you for the gift of life. Thank you for every breath we take; thank you for impregnating us with purpose and the strength to birth that purpose.

In Jesus' precious and mighty name I pray,

AMEN.

INTRODUCTION

There is a period of waiting that we dislike. A period of discomfort, when we want more from life but aren't sure how to attain it. It's difficult to wait for anything, especially in this "I want it now" society, but there's something beautiful about waiting on the Lord. He strengthens where you are weak and prepares you for the battles ahead.

God's love is what most of us are seeking. We feel a desire for something bigger, but don't really know how to identify the missing link. The love of God is not conditional like many of us seem to believe. He loves us despite our shortcomings and our mishaps. Romans 8:38-39 says, "For I am sure that neither death nor life, nor angels nor rulers, nor things present nor things to come, nor powers, nor height nor depth, nor anything else in all creation, will be able to separate us from the love of God in Christ Jesus our Lord." Knowing that nothing can come between the love that God has for me is exciting. God doesn't send us out blindly.

We have the Bible as our playbook, also known as our *Basic Instructions Before Leaving Earth*. God has a plan for each and every one of us.

When people enlist in any branch of the military, they have to go through basic training. It is the training that transforms civilians into soldiers. Have you ever considered that you are in a basic training? We are indeed in spiritual warfare, and there comes a time in each of our lives when we have the opportunity to choose which side of the battle we are on. Are we in the army of God or the forces of God's enemy? Not making a decision is, in fact, a decision. A decision to be neutral, or lukewarm, as the Bible describes it, shows that you are in the army of the evil one. God despises those who are lukewarm. Revelation 3:16 says, "So, because you are lukewarm, and neither hot nor cold, I will spit you out of my mouth."

After we confess that we are in fact desperately in need of being in the Lord's army, we go through *"Basic Training."* During this time, you will learn about patience, courage, humbleness, faithfulness, and how to endure the tough seasons of life. Just as there are drills in basic training, there are drills for this Christian walk of faith. In your basic training, you will be tested. Know that God allows you to retake the test, but if you are in constant conversation with Him and have his word written on your heart, you will pass.

Each chapter in this book details a particular test and provides insightful information about each one. By spending quality time with the Lord, you will learn how He communicates with you. His communication can come through dreams, through His word, through music, through quiet time, through writing what is placed on your heart, or through other people. But no matter how the word comes to you, in developing your relationship with God, you will learn not only about who you are, but who He truly is.

I pray that this book is not only helpful for you, but that it gives you a desire to draw closer to God like never before.

- Ashley

COMFORT ZONE TEST

How to Branch Out and Stand Firm in The Lord

Do you ever wonder if you're settling in life and that you are deserving of more? Have you ever thought that *you* could be the reason that you don't have what you deserve? Often, we are the roadblock in our own way. Becoming the best possible you requires stepping up and out of your comfort zone. It's definitely time to put yourself first and live! Some take life for granted as if it can't be taken in a matter of seconds. Only God knows the exact time of your birth and death. It is up to you to take advantage of the time you have in between.

Instead of focusing on the circumstances, realize that you have a chance to take authority and change your life for the best. It's time to move into your next level of greatness. Your greater is coming! Step aside and receive it.

A comfort zone can become an awkward space. Have you ever said to someone "make yourself comfortable" when they enter your home, but then they become a little too comfortable? We start thinking, when are they going to leave? The concept of being comfortable is simple; you feel safe and content. The problem is that we become complacent, and when God tells us it is time to move, we begin a standoff with Him. We feel entitled to our place of comfort. The topic of comfort zones brings to mind the story of Abram, which begins in Genesis 12. The Lord told Abram to leave his home, his country, and all that he has ever known—his comfort zone.

Most people would come up with every excuse and plead to God with reasons why they can't leave, but Abram asked no questions when following God's command. "Now, the Lord said to Abram, 'Go from your country and your kindred and your father's house to the land that I will show you. And I will make of you a great nation, and I will bless you and make your name great, so that you will be a blessing, I will bless those who bless you, and him who dishonors you I will curse, and in you all the families of the earth shall be blessed'" Genesis 12:1-3. The Lord doesn't disclose where Abram is to go, He just tells him to go and when he gets to the right place God will tell him. Abram takes his wife, Sarai, and his nephew, Lot. Notice in the story, that although God told Abram to leave his kindred, he chose to take his nephew along. When God calls us to do something, it doesn't always include our entourage. Sometimes He just needs you. Lot caused a lot of trouble for Abram later on in the story.

It is extremely important to stand firm in what God has called you to do. A famine came upon the land and Abram, Sarai, and Lot went to Egypt. Here is where trouble begins. Abram told his wife to say she was his sister. He knew that his wife was beautiful and he feared that he would be killed if people knew Sarai was his wife. The result of this untruth was that Pharoah took Sarai as his wife. The Lord sent many plagues because of his act. Soon after, Lot and Abram were forced to separate because the land could not support Abram, Lot, and their possessions. Abram told Lot to choose the land he would inhabit. Lot chose all of the Jordan Valley and moved his tent as far as Sodom.

"The Lord said to Abram, after Lot had separated from him, 'Lift up your eyes and look from the place where you are, northward and southward and eastward and westward, for all the land that you see I will give to you and your offspring forever.'" Genesis 13:14-15

That passage makes it clear that the presence of others can block our blessings. People may not understand when you separate yourself from them. They may talk about you negatively, they may spread rumors, and they may stop talking to you, but it is okay. When doing kingdom business, you are on an assignment, not to gain popularity or to make your name great, but to glorify the Lord and make his name great. There's this notion that people need to know us, remember us, and want to be us, when the truth is that they need to know our maker and savior.

As much as we would like for things to be all about us, they are not. But what is awesome to know is that through the ridicule and the lonely times, we have a faithful friend in Jesus. Never be afraid to stand firm in what you believe and the promises that God has given. There is a lesson to be learned about faith and obedience from Abram.

LESSON #1:

When God says, "Go" You GO!

There are no shortcuts on the journey of fulfilling your purpose. Doing things our way can prolong the process. We get restless and want the formula to success or the secret to how someone "made it," but what God has for you is for you alone. Your journey may look similar to someone else's, but your journey is *your* journey. What someone else did may not play out the same for you, so be confident in what God put inside of you. Know that God created you on purpose and for a purpose. This life is *yours* and the journey you are on is not about anyone else. We must learn to not take on other people's expectations of us. The reality is that they may be forcing us to do something that truly has nothing to do with us, but everything to do with them. It is okay to put you first. Stand firm on what God has revealed to you and pray for Godly boldness in standing firm on that foundation.

When Abram went to Egypt because of the famine in Canaan, he had no reason to be fearful because God protects His people and Abram was on an assignment. God would not allow him to be harmed, yet Abram took his focus off of God and focused on himself, like many of us do in certain situations. We follow and have faith in what God told us until we enter the room with prestigious people in it, then we begin to replay each prayer and each response we thought God gave. The spirit of fear, confusion, and worry are not of God. We must be careful about what we allow ourselves to think and feel. There are consequences when we don't own our truth. The truth is that the Lord is in control and protects His children. We must guard our hearts with the words of the Lord and prepare ourselves so that when things arise, we get a red flag and immediately speak to it and cast it out. We have power given to us by the Lord to speak against things that can bring us harm. Activate your faith and know the power that God has given you.

LESSON #2:

Stay true to who God says you are.

When we take it upon ourselves to bring others along on our journey, who have no place where we are going, chaos eventually breaks out. God is trying to purge us of the things and people who aren't good for us. It is human nature to want to do all and be all for those we care about, but the trouble with that is people begin to solely depend on you and not God. They run to you for every little thing and you eventually become drained. Save yourself the headache and long phone bill. When people come to you with an issue, don't listen so you can solve the problem. Go before the Lord in prayer; intercede for that individual. God hears individual prayers, but the word in Matthew 18:20 says, "Where two or three are gathered in my name, there am I among them." This verse should not be taken lightly; there is power in coming together before the Lord.

Whether praying with one another or on someone else's behalf, God hears our prayers, counts our tears, and knows our fears. We must give Him our all, and trust that He is working everything out for our good.

We must accept that elevation requires separation. This doesn't mean that you should start calling all of your family and friends to tell them you have to separate from them, but you must separate yourself from those who are not moving in a positive direction. Just because you played double-dutch and hide-and-seek with someone doesn't automatically qualify them to be a part of your life forever. God has people who are going to help you fulfill your purpose and grow in Him in a mighty way. Don't feel bad or get distracted because someone is trying to plan a guilt trip for you. Do not pack your bags and go on the trip. We have to pray that God delivers us from people. We are to love one another and build each other up in the name of the Lord, not babysit feelings because someone is afraid to grow.

People that know us before we are "awake" to the true meaning of life and are souled out for Jesus, sometimes have a hard time seeing us in a different light. They tend to judge us based upon who we used to be, so we must learn to believe the word of God. "Therefore, if anyone is in Christ, he is a new creation. The old has passed away; behold, the new has come" 2 Corinthians 5:17. This one verse explains the change that many cannot fathom after professing Jesus as their Lord and Savior. It is the answer when someone asks why you're so different. Seek God for how to interact with people who don't understand the "new" you; He will lead and guide you. Remember you were created to stand out, not conform.

LESSON #3:

NO guilt trippin,' God has you covered.

It is imperative to put the pressure that comes along with life on the shoulders of the one that can truly handle it ALL. We must be intentional to not bog ourselves down with the tests and trials we face on this journey. God is our present help. We tend to think God isn't interested in the "little things," but can I be honest and let you know that EVERYTHING is little to God? God wants us to be in such a close relationship with Him that we talk to Him more than twice a day. The past is indeed the past, your present is here and your future depends on the choices that are made today. Break the lease on your comfort zone and walk in your purpose.

THE WAIT TEST

How to Grow Your Patience
Through Uncomfortable Seasons

How many of us pray for certain things, yet we are impatient and begin to move at our own pace? How many of us are asking of things from others and wanting it now? The key to life is not demands or expectations. It is the process in which things happen. I'm genuinely confused by those who want a mansion and six cars right now, but haven't done the work to achieve them. Some of us want to acquire without doing what is required, but life is a journey.

On the path to acquiring what you want, you learn a lot, you experience things, and most importantly, you live! Enjoy the journey to get to where you want to be in life.

It is time to part with unrealistic expectations and seeking for others to do what you need to do for yourself. It gets lonely and just plain hard at times, but know that your purpose is more important than your circumstances.

This will probably be your least favorite test, but when doing kingdom work, you sometimes have to do things you'd rather not do. For this test we are going to look at Josephs' story which begins in Genesis 37. Joseph's story is one of the greatest underdog stories ever. He was a man of courage and unlimited faith. He had a lot of haters, as we say today. That didn't distract or deter Joseph from pursuing his purpose, but the people that hated Joseph weren't strangers, they were his own brothers. None of the brothers liked Joseph because they were jealous of him and believed that their father showed favoritism toward him. But his brothers' hate grew stronger after Joseph had a dream of greatness, and shared it with them. He also shared another dream with his father who rebuked him. One day, Joseph was sent by his father to check on his brothers and the pasturing flock.

Without question Joseph went. When they saw him coming toward them, they plotted to kill Joseph. Reuben, the oldest of Jacob's twelve sons, stood up and protected him from being murdered by his brothers, and instead of killing Joseph they threw him into a pit and left him there. Genesis 37:21 says, "But when Reuben heard of it, he rescued him out of their hands, saying, 'let us not take his life.'" Thank God for Reuben! He planned to rescue Joseph out of the pit and return him to their father. But while the brothers were having lunch they saw a caravan passing by, and decided to sell Joseph to the Ishmaelites. At this time, Joseph was seventeen years old. How many people, at the age of seventeen, could have handled what Joseph endured? And this was only the beginning.

It is important for us not to get discouraged because of where we start. *Start* is the keyword. Your starting point and your finishing point should be very different, especially If Jesus is your focus. Joseph didn't complain, he didn't go against where God was taking him. I guarantee that Joseph had no idea how his situation would work out for his good, but he pressed through. Instead of grumbling and demanding God to release him from this struggle, he trusted in God and had faith that everything would work out how God saw fit. You see, like Joseph, our lives are filled with tests and trials. We should focus not on the storm, but on the fact that every storm runs out of rain.

LESSON #1:

There is a lesson to be learned from every situation.

Joseph was sold in Egypt to Potipher, who was an officer of Pharaoh and the captain of the guard. The ESV study Bible says, "The Lord was with Joseph. Joseph's life in Egypt is governed by God's providential care." This is evident in Genesis 39: 2-3, "The Lord was with Joseph, and he became a successful man, and he was in the house of his Egyptian master. His master saw that the Lord was with him and that the Lord caused all that he did to succeed in his hands."

No matter what you go through, the Lord is with you and will see you through. Joseph was promoted to overseer of the house. Just how God's hand was all over Joseph's life, it is over your life as well. Potipher's wife became interested in Joseph, but he remained faithful to God and denied her. Potipher's wife lied to Potipher, saying that Joseph slept with her against her will. Potipher immediately had Joseph sent to prison.

Eventually Joseph was put in charge of all the prisoners because God was still with him and showing him favor. Joseph's story is proof that, even in the worst places, you are sanctified and should do the work of our Heavenly Father. Although, Joseph ended up in jail for something he did not do, God was at work.

There are many times when we find ourselves in uncomfortable places, and it's a hard thing to understand. Know that God may have had to move you because you wouldn't obey Him. You got too comfortable. God gives us chance after chance to obey and take heed to His will, and when we don't, He does the moving for us. We have to know that God is for us, and that never changes. Do not allow Satan to plant seeds of fear, confusion, or self-doubt in you. Joshua 1: 9 says, "Have I not commanded you? Be strong and courageous. Do not be frightened, and do not be dismayed for the Lord your God is with you wherever you go." Write this verse down; remember this was written for you. Joseph, at a very young age, was placed into difficult situations that could have hardened his heart toward God, yet he remained faithful and never let a circumstance dictate his faith, praise, or promise.

LESSON #2:

No matter where God has you, He has you.

Soon the Chief Cupbearer and the Chief Baker were sent to prison for offenses they committed. They both had dreams and looked troubled. When Joseph asked them what was wrong, they told Joseph that they both had dreams and no one to interpret them. Joseph asked that the men share their dreams with him; he understood that interpretations belong to God. Dreams were often viewed as divine revelation. The Cupbearer's dream was interpreted to mean that, in three days, he would be back to work and his normal duties, and Joseph asked that once he was back to work for Pharaoh, that he mention Joseph and how he helped him. The Baker then decided to let Joseph interpret his dream since the Cupbearer's dream was good.

Joseph interpreted that the Baker's dream meant that he would die. In three days, Joseph's interpretation proved true. The Chief Cupbearer was sent back to his work and the Chief Baker was hanged. But it was two years before the Chief Cupbearer would do as Joseph had asked. Pharaoh had a dream, and no one could interpret it. It was then that the Chief Cupbearer remembered how Joseph interpreted his dream and the dream of the Chief Baker. He told Pharaoh how the young Hebrew had interpreted their dreams and that all of it had come to pass. Pharaoh sent for Joseph.

Joseph *prepared himself*, shaving and changing his clothes before seeing Pharaoh. Joseph knew he was representing God and made sure he went before Pharaoh presentable. Know that you are the king's kid. You are royalty and should present yourself as such at all times. Pharaoh asked Joseph about the dreams he interpreted for the baker and cupbearer, and Joseph explained that it was not him, but God, who interpreted the dreams. Pharaoh tells his dream to Joseph, who interpreted it. Pharaoh then told Joseph that he will have power over his house and over all the people. You see, Joseph didn't brag or boast about his interpretations because he knew it was God that gave him wisdom of how to interpret the dreams of each man. God deserves total glory for every part of your story. Joseph's humble heart is something to be admired in a world full of selfish motives.

LESSON #3:

Be Prepared! God is working it all out.

Joseph, like many of us, endured many struggles, hardships, and moments where it seemed as if he was abandoned. But throughout everything he endured, he still kept his faith in God. He trusted God's plan and, through it all, he not once complained or questioned God. The key to the wait test is to prepare while you wait. Don't wait idle for God. While you wait on the Lord to open doors, get ready. Stay in His word, develop an intimate prayer life, and strengthen your relationship with the Lord.

There are moments when we feel like God and everyone else has abandoned us, but it is important to know that the teacher is always quiet during a test. Keep grounded on God's word and speak life over yourself and your situation. We literally see God working in Joseph's life, yet it is so easy to forget that He is doing the same for us. The world we live in is bogged down with negativity. Know that no matter how dark it gets and how lonely you feel you are never alone. Joseph went from the pit to the palace. He knew he was exactly where he was supposed to be. You are exactly where you are for a purpose as well.

"Wait for the Lord; be strong, and let your heart take courage; wait for the Lord!" Psalm 27:14

THE COURAGE TEST

How to Boldly Stand Firm on the Word of God

"Too many people undervalue what they are and overvalue what they're not." – Anonymous

Being you should be easy! But some people feel like they have to keep up with the "Jones's" in order to be accepted or taken seriously, yet being yourself should attract people that genuinely care for you, people that really have your best interest at heart. Do yourself a favor and be you! Accept who you are and who you are trying to become, and let no one stand in your way. If you are comfortable with what others may perceive to be shortcomings, the urge to put on a facade will be nonexistent.

We all have moments when we wish we could take off the mask and reveal who we truly are and how we feel. We fear that people won't like us, or that they will judge us. This is a test of courage because those from whom we hide ourselves are not the people we need in our lives. God knows what and who we need. He is the ultimate provider, and when we rely totally on Him, there is no limit to what we can do and become. When I think of someone of courage, I think of Moses. His life wasn't ordinary and he wasn't the most confident, but the Lord helped him to be courageous. He learned that he could do nothing in his own power, but with God all things are possible.

When we look at the story of Moses, found in the book of Exodus, we learn that our strength and help really does come solely from the Lord, and that we must simply get out of our own way and let him lead us. During the time of Moses' birth, the Pharaoh wanted all infant male Hebrew children to be killed. Pharaoh feared that there were too many Hebrew people and if things ever went wrong, they could rise against him and overthrow his kingdom. Moses' mother hid him for three months, then put him in a basket and placed it in the river. Baby Moses was discovered by Pharaoh's daughter, who raised him, giving him the name Moses because she drew him out of water. As Moses grew, he saw how badly the Egyptians were treating the Hebrew people and one day witnessed an Egyptian beating a Hebrew. He killed the Egyptian. Moses left once news spread about what he had done to the Egyptian man. He fled to Midian and found himself in an unfamiliar space in every aspect.

Moses sat next to a well and the priest of Midian's seven daughters were sent to the well to draw water for their father's flock. The daughters were driven away by shepherds, but Moses stood up for them and even drew the water for them. He eventually married one of the daughters, Zipporah, and they had a son. Although Moses did something terrible, he knew that the treatment of the Hebrew people was not okay, making his story one of courage and redemption. He soon learned that once God qualifies you for greater, that is the only approval you need.

LESSON #1:

Never be afraid to stand firmly for what is right, or good.

Moses tended to his father-in-law's flock, and led it west of the wilderness to a place called Horeb, "the mountain of God." Exodus 3:2-6 says "And the angel of the Lord appeared to him in a flame of fire out of the midst of a bush. He looked, and behold, the bush was burning, yet it was not consumed. And Moses said, 'I will turn aside to see this great sight, why the bush is not burned.' When the Lord saw that he turned aside to see, God called to him out of the bush, 'Moses, Moses!' And he said, 'Here I am.' Then he said, 'Do not come near; take your sandals off your feet, for the place on which you are standing is holy ground.' And he said, 'I am the God of your father, the God of Abraham, the God of Isaac, and the God of Jacob.' And Moses hid his face, for he was afraid to look at God."

In reading those verses, we notice that God came by fire, but he didn't come with wrath. God took notice of the oppression of the Hebrew people that were in Egypt. Exodus 3:8 says, "and I have come down to deliver them out of that land to a good and broad land, a land flowing with milk and honey, to the place of the Canaanites, the Hittities, the Amorites, the Perizzites, the Hivites, and the Jebusites." Exodus 3:10 reads "Come, I will send you to Pharaoh that you may bring my people, the children of Israel, out of Egypt." Immediately Moses questions Gods plan. In Exodus 3:11-12 Moses asks God, "who am I that I should go to Pharaoh and bring the children of Israel out of Egypt."

God replied "But I will be with you, and this shall be the sign for you, that I have sent you: when you have brought the people out of Egypt, you shall serve God on this mountain."

How many of us know the Lord has called us to do something great, but because of our past or because of our comfort zone we self-doubt and disqualify ourselves? The fact that God is always with us should be reason enough to walk by faith daily and know that His promises are more than true.

LESSON #2:

BELIEVE what God says about you in his word.

Moses wasn't convinced that he could actually free the Hebrew people from Pharaoh. He came up with question after question and excuse after excuse. Exodus 4:1 says "Then Moses answered, 'But behold, they will not believe me or listen to my voice, for they will say, 'the Lord did not appear to you.'" God ensured Moses that He would be with Him, but Moses was focused on what He could accomplish in his own will. In our own will, we are capable of absolutely nothing. When God gives us an assignment, there is no need to fear or worry. Allow God to be God. He will show up and fulfill exactly what He said he would.

Sometimes, it's difficult to walk out something the Holy Spirit placed on your heart. Other people won't always understand your assignment and you cannot expect them to because God gave it to you. Despite how difficult things can get, when people start to doubt you or brush you off, you have to unapologetically represent God just as we unapologetically represent things of the world. We spend money to represent people we don't even know, people who have done nothing for us, but contemplate whether or not to tell others how Jesus protected us, healed us, or provided for us.

In Exodus 4:10 Moses spoke to the Lord, saying "Oh, my Lord, I am not eloquent, either in the past or since you have spoken to your servant, but I am slow of speech and of tongue." If the Lord is sovereign and all knowing, it is safe to assume that he knows our shortcomings and flaws. He chooses to use us despite the things we lack, which is why He gets His glory. We can never take total credit for anything because we are an imperfect people, but with God we are made whole. Moses counted himself out although was conversing with God himself.

We have the tendency to put ourselves on the bench of life because of things we perceive as weaknesses.

We think, "There is no way I can really do this." God is saying, "Trust in me." We say we trust with our mouths far more than we show it with our lives. Exodus 4:11 "The Lord said to him, "Who has made man's mouth? Who makes him mute, or deaf, or seeing, or blind? Is it not I, the Lord?" God created you and knows everything about you, and still wants to use you.

LESSON #3:

Know that you are equipped for all that God has for you.

We overthink every detail when we need to activate our faith and start walking what we talk. We talk to others about how awesome and great our God is, yet when things get uncomfortable, we act as though we are of the world. We have to choose to die for ourselves daily. It is not easy, but it is worth it. We will see God's plan and His provision manifest if we get off of the bench and get in this game of life. We must stand firmly on the word of God, regardless of the circumstance; know that He is with you.

"Beloved, do not be surprised at the fiery trial when it comes upon you to test you, as though something strange were happening to you. But rejoice insofar as you share Christ's sufferings, that you may also rejoice and be glad when his glory is revealed" 1 Peter 4:12-13.

THE STUDY TEST

*Being in Your Word, Hungry to Learn
and Eager to Grow Closer to God*

n order to get to a better place in life, you have to overcome some things. In order to grow, there will be a struggle. I once felt a tug-of-war going on within myself. My spirit and my mind were battling. I was at a place of growth and elevation, so a lot of the things I used to think, say, do, or feel had no place in me any longer. God was starting to truly purge me of everything that had to go, and the only thing I could do was pray. I didn't understand what was happening or how to explain. I felt like I was settling in life, just going through the motions.

I now understand that by operating at a lower level, I was simply helping the devil. Now that I was truly getting into position, he and his minions were not pleased at all.

When we don't operate in the capacity in which God created us to, we aren't a threat. The more I prayed and spent time reading my Bible, the harder Satan tried to deter me from moving forward, but I was determined to elevate and grow my spirit. I was at bible study weekly, Sunday service, and every conference or fellowship I could find. I was desperate to grow closer to God and to be in His presence with other believers. Christian life is not perfect, and we all go through trials and hardships; those hardships have a way of keeping you humble. The faith that we have in God to see and strengthen us through the struggle is what gives us the ability to overcome. God does everything with purpose. You can overcome anything in your way! With God, ALL things are possible.

"Listen! Behold, a sower went out to sow. And as he sowed, some seed fell along the path, and the birds came and devoured it. Other seed fell on rocky ground, where it did not have much soil, and immediately it sprang up, since it had no depth of soil, and when the sun rose, it was scorched, and since it had no root, it withered away. Other seed fell among thorns, and the thorns grew up and choked it, and it yielded no grain. And other seeds fell into good soil and produced grain, growing up and increasing and yielding thirtyfold and sixtyfold and a hundredfold." And he said, 'He who has ears to hear let him hear.'" Mark 4:3-9

In order for anything to grow, it must have the correct environment, proper nutrients, and a firm foundation. It is safe to say that a lot of us are in places we don't belong because our foundation isn't beneficial to our growth. The scripture above gives every reason why the seed grew, died, or prospered. Some seeds fell and were devoured by birds before they were able to be planted. God plants seeds in us, but we allow them to be devoured by others.

We give people too much power and expect God to be God, but in reality we have made people our God. We have to take back the authority we have given to people and truly know and believe that what God says about us is true. Other seeds fell on rocky ground and immediately sprang up. This applies to those of us who are impatient and just refuse to trust God's timing. The foundation is not stable, yet we cut corners and try to help God be God. We try to take matters into our own hands, and then cry out to God when relationships fail, business deals fall through, our car gets repossessed, or our house is in foreclosure. We have to wait on the Lord and trust His perfect timing.

The seed that landed on rocky ground, yes it sprang up immediately, but was scorched and died because its roots weren't deep enough. The outcome looked promising, but soon it died, and bared no fruit. When the heat gets turned up do you shut down? We run out into this unforgiving world thinking we know it all and can do it all in our own strength, and we get scorched like that seed that sprang up. We get hurt by people, lose hope, get used and abused, and come limping back to God to repair afflictions that could have been avoided if we stayed anchored in Christ. This cycle of hurt and the depreciation of our self-worth can be avoided through conversation with God.

Other seeds fell among thorns and the thorns choked them. Is your circle of friends pushing you toward God, or are they choking you? Are they holding you back, keeping you in a box that makes them feel comfortable with being stagnant and complacent? We hold ourselves back because we don't want to offend others, but if they truly love and care for you, they won't condemn you for wanting better for your life. People have a tendency to transfer insecurities. Pray that God surrounds you with the people you need, not the people you want. The other seeds fell into good soil and produced grain.

Imagine what you can produce when you get into position. The Lord is waiting on you so that He can bless you, but remember that once you give your life to Christ, this does not mean that you are immediately "fixed" and ready to save other souls. The reality is that the moment you give your life to Christ, you make the decision to face your demons and clean house. God purges us of the things of the world; we have to earnestly pray to be renewed. We've grown accustomed to loving things of the world, and some things will still have a hold on us. There are some worldly things that we have planted in good soil, and we have to work to uproot the weeds that have kept us bound and away from Christ.

In order to grow into our purpose, we must lay the foundation. That foundation consists of a genuine prayer life, establishing a relationship with Christ, reading our Bibles and holding onto the truth therein, allowing God to use us how He sees fit, submitting to the will of God, dying to ourselves daily, and trusting God through the process. Preparation isn't always pretty, but it's necessary.

LESSON #1:

Lay the Foundation.

In this world that seems to be moving at an incredibly fast pace, it's easy to get overwhelmed with deadlines, events, appointments, and meetings, and if you have children, that list multiplies. It seems like the world is working against us and demanding so much of our time that we feel like we have to pencil in time for God. Beware of distractions. Despite how hectic our daily schedule is, the God we serve is with us at all times, so whether we talk to him while walking into work or while driving home, He hears us.

We must be intentional in what we do, say, think, and even feel. We have to do more than try to spend time with the Lord and truly nurture and develop the relationship like all of our others. A lot of people say, "I'm trying," but trying means nothing without intent. It is imperative for us to do more than just try. We have to be intentional about being intentional. We must be sure that we aren't just talking to talk, but that we are putting forth the necessary effort to achieve the goal we set out to accomplish. God continually gives us His very best, and we sometimes unintentionally overlook all He has done on our behalf because we're too busy being busy. We are not here to be busy, but to intentionally work to expand the kingdom. "But seek first the Kingdom of God and his righteousness, and all these things will be added to you" Matthew 6:33.

The verse says, "seek first the Kingdom." A lot of us miss that point, seeking people, alcohol, drugs, food, and other things to fill voids in our lives, instead of the one that can totally fill it. We have to be intentional about seeking God first. When your time comes to leave this Earth, there will be no Instagram, Facebook, Twitter, or any other social media outlet to fill the time gaps with. It is important to not get caught up in religion but caught up in relationship with God.

LESSON #2:

Be INTENTIONAL.

"Your word is a lamp to my feet and a light to my path." Psalm 119:105

The Lord's word is a lamp unto our feet (guiding us) and a light unto our path (leading us). God doesn't intend for us to be lost and confused, trying to navigate through this life alone. He wants to be on this journey with us. We cannot get so busy that we forget why we are here. We each have a purpose and God has a plan. Jeremiah 29:11 says "For I know the plans I have for you,' declares the Lord, 'plans to prosper you and not harm you, plans to give you hope and a future.'" Nothing can compare to the unwavering love of God.

We search for something real, but try not to get too deep with God because we lack self-control and are afraid that if we make mistakes, people will talk. There is power in living for God. People mocked Jesus, and they will mock you. You are in a battle and everyday won't be sunshine and rainbows, but what God has in store for you is worth every single tear that you have shed. We have to prepare for battle. It would be great to have a list of what we need to be prepared, right? God graciously gave us one!

Ephesians 6:10-18.

"Finally, be strong in the Lord and in the strength of his might. Put on the whole armor of God that you may be able to stand against the schemes of the devil. For we do not wrestle against flesh and blood, but against the rulers, against the authorities, against the cosmic powers over this present darkness, against the spiritual forces of evil in the heavenly places.

*Therefore take up the whole armor of God that you may be able to withstand in the evil day, and having fastened on **the belt of truth**, and having put on the **breastplate of righteousness**, and as shoes for your feet, having put* *on the readiness given by **the gospel of peace**. In all circumstances take up the **shield of faith**, with which you can extinguish all the flaming darts of the evil one; and take the **helmet of salvation,** and **the sword of the spirit**, <u>which is the word of God,</u> praying at all times in the spirit, with all prayer and supplication. To that end keep with all perseverance, making supplication for all the saints"*

LESSON #3:

Set your focus on the Lord.

I'll be honest and say that I never truly learned how to study in school, none of my teachers taught us. I couldn't use that as an excuse when it was time to take an exam to say, "You didn't teach me to study" and leave the paper blank. That was not an option. I had to intentionally make time to review what was necessary and in some cases learn concepts. Each of us are responsible for our lives, it is our responsibility to ensure that we do whatever it takes to be prepared. There are no excuses, no blaming your mom or dad, grandma, or anyone else, this life is YOURS! It is time to stop treating our relationships with the Lord as a chore or just something we're supposed to do. Glorifying God is what we were created to do. Stop giving God scraps and submit all of yourself to Him.

No more relying on what has been told to you, we must know God and his word for ourselves. When we do so we begin to understand ourselves. "Be diligent to present yourself approved to God, a worker who does not need to be ashamed, rightly dividing the word of truth." 2 Timothy 2:15

THE TRUST TEST

People vs. God, Learning Where Your Trust Lies

Jesus, full of the Holy Spirit, returned from the Jordan and was led by the Spirit in the desert, where for forty days he was tempted by the devil. He ate nothing during those days, and at the end of them he was hungry. The devil said to him, 'If you are the Son of God, tell this stone to become bread.' Jesus answered, 'It is written: Man does not live on bread alone.' The devil led him up to a high place and showed him in an instant all the kingdoms of the world. And he said to him, 'I will give you all their authority and splendor, for it has been given to me, and I can give it to anyone I want so if you worship me, it will all be yours.' Jesus answered, 'It is written: 'Worship the Lord your God and serve him only'" Luke 4:1-8.

We tend to complain, grumble and ask "why me?" But the real question is "why not me?" If the devil tempted Jesus, what makes you think you are exempt from difficulties in life? The key to being in the midst of a difficult moment or season is knowing the source of your strength. God allows us to be tested so that we may be elevated and trusted with more. We are entitled to live a life of abundance because of God's amazing grace and favor, but we have to be reliable and responsible.

When you were younger and asked for money for the ice cream truck, you weren't given $100. It was understood that you were not responsible enough to be entrusted with that amount of money. It is the same with God. He knows that you are not yet capable of certain things. Trials and tribulations are your training. Not everything will go as you plan because you are not in total control.

Spend more time with God and less time on social networks trying to be someone else. Be patient, have faith, and trust that the Lord will provide and never fail you. Your time is coming. You are not alone, everyone has trials, even Jesus had them, but He was steadfast and did not give in. Stop giving in to what others want you to be and the things they want you to do. To get to a better place in life, you have to overcome some things. Hardships have a way of keeping you humble, and the faith that we have in God is what allows us to overcome them. You may be experiencing a hardship, but it is helping you. God does everything with purpose; trust in Him.

LESSON #1:

Be okay with being human, mistakes will be made. It is how you react and recover that matters.

So many of us have been toe–to-toe with the world and are bruised and broken. We have gotten lost in the chaos and the ideals of what this life is meant to be. So many of us are suffering from an identity crisis. We read the word of God and it says that we are a royal priesthood, but how many of us truly believe? How many of us when reading John 3:16 understand the depths of love that it took for Jesus to die for us?

It can be difficult to understand why God feels how He feels about us because we look at everyone and everything with a jaded view. When you read scripture do you really believe it? Do you personalize it as if God is directly speaking to you? We have to pray that God softens our hearts towards Him and 2 Timothy 3:16 says, "All scripture is breathed out by God and profitable for teaching, for reproof, for correction, and for training in righteousness." This means that everything God says about you is an indisputable fact. No one can take that away. You are who God says you are, and nothing less! We have to believe what God says and accept it because the Lord's love is unconditional and very real. We will never fully understand and know it all, but we do have the Bible to guide us through.

I remember going to church throughout my life, but I didn't become "awake" in church until I was 12. I started to want to know more, and I began being hungry for the word of God. The most important piece of advice that I can offer you is to never just accept what someone tells you about God and His word. You must know for yourself. When reading the Bible, or if you are given a Bible verse, read the text before and after to understand the context.

I strongly encourage you to read the entire chapter. When you hear a sermon or hear someone quote the Bible, fact check for yourself. Your relationship with the

Lord is yours; don't depend on what others "know" about God's word. Believing what the world says is harmful and very dangerous. Stay focused and rooted in the truth. Being rooted in the word builds your relationship and definitely your trust with the Lord. When you have conflicting emotions about certain situations, it may seem like God may be taking too long, but this is where having Christ and knowing the word is essential.

If we have people in our ear giving us advice to handle things on our own terms, without the Lord, you are going to face a challenge that could possibly have been avoided. We can't choose to trust in the Lord only when we have run out of options. He should always be our first option. "And we know that for those who love God all things work together for good, for those who are called according to his purpose" Romans 8:28.

We have to ditch our plans and allow God to work in our lives and use us according to His will. A lot of us are just in the way, trying to be God's assistant manager. We trust him with certain areas of our lives, but refuse to let him have sole custody. He is not the person who hurt you. He is your heavenly father, who sent His son to die for you. He loves and cares for you. It's time to give Him your obedience and trust Him.

Know the word of God for yourself!

"Depart from here and turn eastward and hide yourself by the brook Cherith, which is east of the Jordan. You shall drink from the brook, and I have commanded the ravens to feed you there. So he went and did according to the word of the Lord. He went and lived by the brook Cherith that is east of Jordan. And the ravens brought him bread and meat in the morning, and bread and meat in the evening, and he drank from the brook. And after while the brook dried up because there was no rain in the land"1 Kings 17:3-7.

The Lord told Elijah to go to the brook and Elijah obliged. The Lord told him that He commanded ravens to bring him food. This is where many would have begun to question. Birds take food, they don't share. If you have ever been to City Island in New York, you know those birds are not friendly or willing to give up any scrap of food, but Elijah didn't question the Lord. Elijah trusted God and what He told him to do. God is still working miracles today, just as He did to provide food for Elijah.

God reversed the law of nature to supply Elijah with food. If He did that for Elijah, He is able to come through for you. We compartmentalize God's character to fit our futile way of thinking. The God we serve is capable of any and everything! Our faith in God causes us to accept the unfamiliar and to go a little further, stepping out of the normalcy; we have to trust the Lord wholeheartedly on this journey through life. God has a way of growing our trust and faith in Him. He will put us in a brook situation so that He can show you that He is still God and capable of supplying your needs.

We have to give God glory for everything and every season. He is quick to remind us who He is. Faith is the currency of the Kingdom. When our faith grows, we have more access to kingdom knowledge. He prepares us to go where He needs us to go. God separates us from our normal routines so we can clearly hear His instructions and prepares us for what is to come. We must trust and believe with our total being.

LESSON #3:

Trust in God and His plan for you.

"For I know the plans I have for you,' declares the Lord, 'plans for welfare and not for evil, to give you a future and a hope.'" Jeremiah 29:11 God's plans for the exiles talked about in Jeremiah 29 was for welfare and His plans for you are exactly that. Test and trials cannot and will not break you; activate your faith and put all of your trust in the Lord. His word is true. We are what we speak, and if we continue to say things like "I can't trust anyone" or "I have trust issues," that's exactly what will be.

We have to take all of our issues to the Lord and not apply the issues to our relationship with Him. "For our heart is glad in him, because we trust in his holy name." Psalm 33:21

THE DISCIPLE TEST

Unapologetically Sharing the Word of God

"You did not choose me, but I chose you and appointed you that you should go and bear fruit and that your fruit should abide, so that whatever you ask the Father in my name, he may give it to you"
John 15:16.

If God intended for everyone to be the same, He would have made us so. There's no mistake in the way you were made. You're on this Earth with a specific purpose. I challenge you not to dare to be different, yet dare to be yourself! Be exactly who you are intended to be and learn how to maximize your gifts. You are beautiful, talented, and fearfully created.

Let no one tell you otherwise. We each have an assignment that must be completed.

The enemy once told me I wasn't smart enough to go to a four-year university, that I didn't deserve to be alive, that nobody cared about me, and that I was purposeless. *But God.* He was still calling me even though I tried to ignore Him for years. I didn't understand that God was actually calling me to stand up and step out. Now I talk more about Jesus than I do myself. Sharing the love of God is easy because I truly believe in Him and His love. I've witnessed His work, and I am grateful for being alive this long.

We are called to love others as Christ loves us. When you love people, you can't let them walk in darkness. We are obligated to share the gospel. There are so many people at your school, at your job, in your social circles, in your family, even in your church, walking around screaming on the inside, begging that someone says something so they can spill their truth. I was that person. I would hang on the conversations of others, waiting for a word that identified my feelings and praying that they could feel my brokenness.

Behind my smile, I was torn up, hurt, and feeling lonely and unloved. I was very outspoken and strong with a very bubbly personality, so people just didn't think I was hurt. They could not see it. I remember praying that someone could see my hurt, but it never happened.

God stepped in and began to heal me, and I started to feel like I had a voice that mattered. I felt like I had a purpose; it was as if God renewed my life. We have to open our mouths and help one another. We live in a head down society, and we're taught to keep your phone out so people won't bother you.

When is conversing and connecting with others a social faux pas? We are called to fellowship and build one another up. It is time to stop hiding behind the label Christian and live as such. People brag about what "they" have done or accomplished, but a true believer acknowledges that life is impossible without the Lord. Let your life speak for you.

Share the goodness of the Lord with others, give Him all the glory and honor for bringing you through whatever you went through. "For by grace you have been saved through faith. And this is not your own doing; it is the gift of God, not a result of works, so that no one may boast" Ephesians 2:8-9.

Give Credit Where Credit is Due, All Credit Goes to GOD!

"You are the salt to the earth, but if salt has lost its taste, how shall its saltiness be restored? It is no longer good for anything except to be thrown out and trampled under people's feet. You are the light of the world. A city set on a hill cannot be hidden. Nor do people light a lamp and put it under a basket, but on a stand, and it gives light to all in the house. In the same way, let your light shine before others, so that they may see your good works and give glory to your Father who is in heaven" Matthew 5:13-16.

This verse is calling us out to be who Christ has called us to be, and to rise up and speak truth in a world full of chaos. Salt without taste is pointless. If you don't get into position and start walking in your purpose, you will become tasteless salt and be of no use to the Kingdom. We have the right to unapologetically be who Christ says we are. There is no reason to tiptoe around all that God is doing in you and through you. Never apologize for being that woman or man of God. Some question you and may try to shift their insecurities onto you because they lack the self-control and humility to submit to God, but that is not your problem. You exude confidence when God is at the center of your life; don't apologize for it. Allow God to shine through you, but avoid arrogance or cockiness. Remain humble. Your belief in God, Jesus, and the Holy Spirit should be anchored in your heart. Your beliefs and values are what make you, "you." There are a multitude of believers, but we are all individuals with our own talents and gifts. Own yours. Stay true to your belief in God. It is also important to step away, refocus and spend quiet time with just you and the Lord. Never apologize for needing alone time. The more you abide in Christ, the more you discover your authentic self. It is a process, but being authentically you is something to be admired.

"For he will be great before the Lord. And he must not drink wine or strong drink, and he will be filled with the Holy Spirit, even from his mother's womb." Luke 1:15

Even before His birth, John was called to serve in ministry. He lived and preached in the wilderness of Judea and lived a simple life; he wore clothes made from camel hair and ate locusts and honey. He didn't need much, but he was on fire to share the truth about Jesus. He prepared the way for Jesus by calling people to repent.

"The next day he saw Jesus coming toward him, and said, 'Behold, the Lamb of God, who takes away the sin of the world! This is he of whom I said, 'After me comes a man who ranks before me, because he was before me. I myself did not know him, but for this purpose I came baptizing with water, that he might be revealed to Israel.' And John bore witness: 'I saw the Spirit descend from heaven like a dove, and it remained on him. I myself did not know him, but he who sent me to baptize with water said to me, 'He on whom you see the Spirit descend and remain, this is he who baptizes with the Holy Spirit.' And I have seen and have borne witness that this is the Son of God.'" John 1:29-34

John was unashamed of what he knew about Jesus, and he unapologetically did as the spirit moved him. We should admire his discernment to truly be who God created him to be. He didn't need material things; all he needed was the truth that was written on his heart.

LESSON #2:

Be who God says you are, unapologetically you.

"Go therefore and make disciples of all nations, baptizing them in the name of the Father and of the Son and of the Holy Spirit, teaching them to observe all that I have commanded you. And behold, I am with you always, to the end of the age." Matthew 28: 19-20

It is our duty to share the truth about God. As much as we try to make life about ourselves and our own happiness, it is not about us. We have been saved and changed to help others along the way. The enemy wants us to be isolated and to go through life with blinders on, not genuinely caring about those around us, but we are here to help one another.

"Not neglecting to meet together, as is the habit of some, but encouraging one another, and all the more as you see the Day drawing nearing." Hebrews 10:25

We are to gather in fellowship with one another, to walk this life with those that support where God is leading us, not to gossip and place one another on false pedestals. We tend to overcomplicate simple matters such as discipleship because we get selfish and want to hold onto that good thing from God as if He is our personal genie. God will never run out of blessings, lessons, or tests. He is the creator of all things, and the more you give, the more you receive. Sometimes God will use you without your knowledge. You can say something in a casual conversation that can confirm the very thing someone was praying for the night before.

We have to always be prepared and ready to give to others. We have to live lives modeled after Christ. No we will never be perfect. We will make mistakes, but God's grace abounds and He is our redeemer. People watch and see how much you have overcome and are flabbergasted at how you are still standing. God picks up where we lack and because of His son, we are made whole. It is time to boldly proclaim God and live out loud for Him. The best gift you can give to someone is the gospel and the truth about our Heavenly Father.

LESSON #3:

Live OUTLOUD and PROUD for God, SHARE the good news!

"And we impart this in words not taught by human wisdom but taught by the spirit, interpreting spiritual truths to those who are spiritual." 1 Corinthians 2:13 Every person that professes Jesus Christ as their personal Lord and Savior and declares they are a Christian is to be not only led but empowered by the Holy Spirit. Allow the Holy Spirit to have His way and do His job in leading you. I ask the Holy Spirit everything from what I should wear to what to say. A true disciple allows room for God in every aspect (Father, Son, Holy Spirit) to be God.

THE LIFE TEST

Putting God First Daily and Seeking Him Earnestly

"Do not be conformed to this world, but be transformed by the renewal of your mind, that by testing you may discern what is the will of God, what is good and acceptable and perfect"
Romans 12:2

A lot of us struggle with things from our past, "skeletons" in our closets, things we have swept under the rug, but those things get heavy. Burdens, despair, rejection, rape, feelings of being unloved, loneliness, sickness, generational curses, daddy issues, mommy issues, all become heavy on your heart, mind, and soul.

It is time to find a way to let it all go and to stop holding on to negative situations and negative people. Get it out and let it go so you can grow! Holding grudges or keeping things to yourself hurts you more than anything else. Be brave enough to fight for the things you deserve. Don't let the past determine your future. Stand up and fight! Things that have happened to you do not define you. Things happen in life, but what matters is being and doing better. If something or someone is toxic, it is time to drop that burden. Take the limits off. Do whatever is necessary to better yourself.

I see you standing with your head up. Keep taking off those burdens. We get hurt, we get knocked down, and we get upset, but our God is a healer. We try to heal ourselves or seek others to heal our hurts, but it will never work. God heals us in a way that truly forces us to get to the root of the issue. God didn't leave you when you assumed He did. He has a "hands on" way of teaching and He expects that you will use your trials as a testament. That testament requires that you endure life's trials. Someone who speaks from experience has much more to offer to someone who has been in a similar situation. What you endured was not just for your growth. After you have sought the Lord and He has healed and renewed you, it is time to work. Healing precedes helping.

Once you identify the issue and handle business with the Lord, you must then help others. This is a crucial piece to seeking the Lord and having a heart after His will. We are living in a fallen world, but we serve a God who equips us with the necessities to do our part in kingdom building. Our heavenly father prepares us for the battles we will face, so He pulls us aside and strips us of the distractions we have allowed to take precedence over Him in our lives. In doing so, He renews us, and as we grow in Him, our hearts desire things that are like Him. We begin to be more like him. Allow God to heal you and rest knowing that you are not your past. It is time to let it go.

LESSON #1:

Let Go to Grow

"Put to death therefore what is earthly in you: sexual immorality, impurity, passion, evil desire, and covetousness, which is idolatry. On account of these the wrath of God is coming. In these you too once walked, when you were living in them. But now you must put them all away: anger, wrath, malice, slander, and obscene talk from your mouth. Do not lie to one another, seeing that you have put off the old self with its practices" Colossians 3:5-10

We must be aware of our thoughts and see distractions for what they are. Being aware will save you a lot of time and pain. Don't allow your blessings to be blocked because you are too busy being jealous of someone else's. What God has for you is already written. "If I only had..." is a phrase that can set you up, set you back, or keep you from moving forward. When you find yourself with those thoughts, simply say, "Thank you Lord for all that I have. Thank you for what you have done, are doing now, and are about to do."

You have to train your mind. When you are in the world, but not of the world, distractions are everywhere. Focus is critical because your mind is a war zone at times. But the fight is worth fighting. Don't quit. Put yourself into a position to win in life. Do not just exist, live. Time isn't waiting for you.

"Be sober-minded; be watchful. Your adversary the devil prowls around like a roaring lion, seeking someone to devour" 1 Peter 5:8

We have to be intentional about guarding our hearts and minds. We have to discern who we follow on social media, who we are around in our daily lives, what we read, watch on television, and the music we listen to. God made all things, but all things do not glorify Him. We must make a steady effort to glorify Him in all that we do. There are days when we are just not feeling it, bogged down or even just a little lost, but God will pick you up. He makes the impossible, possible.

The goal is not to live a perfect life, but to live a life that glorifies a perfect God. We are the church; we represent our father. You would never intentionally do something that would bring dishonor to your family name, so it should be the same for God because we are His children. We must serve Christ alone, not our comfort zones and our own motives. We have to be focused and intentional. The enemy knows the areas where you are lacking and will tempt you, but if you are seeking God and growing in the relationship with Him, the Holy Spirit will alert you.

LESSON #2:

Guard Yourself

"Not everyone who says to me, 'Lord, Lord,' will enter the kingdom of heaven, but the one who does the will of my Father who is in heaven. On that day many will say to me, 'Lord, Lord, did we not prophesy in your name, and cast out demons in your name, and do many mighty works in your name?' And then will I declare to them, 'I never knew you; depart from me, you workers of lawlessness.'" Matthew 7:21-23

This verse has the power to hurt feelings. If we are not genuinely seeking the Lord and trusting His will for our lives, all of this earthly work will be in vain. Religion teaches us to do things out of routine, but seeking Christ is about a relationship. Like any relationship, we must spend time with Him and learn Him for ourselves. It is not enough to do things because our parent or guardian says so. It is not enough to hang on to the words of a pastor or spiritual leader.

We have to know God for ourselves and genuinely do what is necessary to surrender and submit to His will. Your purpose may require that you let some things and some people go. In order to elevate we have to lighten the load. Your purpose is tailor-made and doesn't make you a bad person; it makes you a great example.

"Now as they went on their way, Jesus entered a village. And a woman named Martha welcomed him into her house. And she had a sister called Mary, who sat at the Lord's feet and listened to his teaching. But Martha was distracted with much serving. And she went up to him and said, 'Lord, do you not care that my sister has left me to serve alone? Tell her then to help me.' But the Lord answered her, 'Martha, Martha, you are anxious and troubled about many things, but one thing is necessary. Mary has chosen the good portion, which will not be taken away from her.'" Luke 10:38-42

Martha was busy being busy, while Mary made time to listen and submit to the Lord's teaching. We cannot simply bombard the Lord with words; we must also wait and listen earnestly to what He has to say.

LESSON #3:

Busyness is a distraction and does not excuse the need for relationship.

"Look carefully then how you walk, not as unwise but as wise, making the best use of the time, because the days are evil. Therefore do not be foolish, but understand what the will of the Lord is." Ephesians 5:15-17 Understand that God is not impressed by how full your calendar is, especially if all that you do is to glorify yourself. Do everything with purpose, love, and zeal. Do things that edify others and build up the kingdom of God. Learn to say "no" to some things as well. We tend to feel obligated to bend and twist to do something, and we forget to go before God for direction. Now, schedules are important. The point here is not to throw out your day planner, yet to be conscious of the day you plan. The verse above says "making the best use of the time." The best use of time is when you are doing something God told you to do. Pray and seek Him first.

THE PURPOSE TEST

God Reveals What He Calls You to Do

"Agree with God, and be at peace; thereby good will come to you." **Job 22:21**

At one point, I felt like I was battling between myself and what God needed of me. I felt as though I was in my own way, holding myself back. I'm sure many of you may have felt that same feeling, as if you're trying to get to the next level, but you can't because the mess you have made for yourself is in the way. I prayed for God to wreck me and the plans I had for my life (and He didn't wait a minute). I realized the things and people that I wanted were not what I needed.

Growing in Christ, I have learned that there is a big difference between needs and wants. Before, I was all about my wants, but now, before I do anything, I ask God "Is this going to benefit you and your kingdom?" I make a conscious effort to go to my heavenly father with everything. When you are on a path and walking in your purpose, there are some things that must change before the journey continues. There are some people that must get off the trail and there are some thoughts that must get off as well. What are the habits, thoughts, people, or activities that God needs to "wreck" and rid you of? Ask him!

Make it clear. He already knows the desires of our hearts, but we must do our part. I knew for a long time that I was different and that there was something on my life that I could feel, but could not put it into words. I did everything to run away, but there was no running and no hiding. Eventually, I had to accept the call on my life and walk in it.

Developing a relationship with our heavenly father is the best relationship investment. We invest time, money and energy into people who can only do so much for us, but the moment we give our whole hearts to God, there is no greater love we will experience. I challenge you to write down what you feel needs to be "wrecked" so you can be restored and aligned with your greater.

"Whoever finds his life will lose it, and whoever loses his life for my sake will find it."- Matthew 10:30

The verse above may be short in length, but is loaded with wisdom and truth, saying that a life that you find in your own willpower will cost you, and a life submitted to God's will be one that is blessed and prosperous. You can be alive, yet dead mentally, emotionally, and spiritually. Physically you're still breathing, but your life isn't producing what is needed to bring joy and fulfillment.

God graciously gives us free will to choose how we do things, but we have to be conscious and decide whether certain things or people have taken precedence over God in our lives.

LESSON #1:

Assess Your Priorities; Are You Living to Glorify God or Yourself?

When on the journey to understand your purpose or to pursue your purpose, you must be prepared to fight. "For we do not wrestle against flesh and blood, but against the rulers, against authorities, against the cosmic powers over this present darkness, against the spiritual forces of evil in the heavenly places." Ephesians 6:12

We will never live the life we were truly created to live if we show up for battle with the wrong tools. We have to recognize the war we are fighting. It is not just a war of the flesh; it is spiritual. As we submit to God daily, we must ask Him to grow our spirit. Many people are living in bondage because they aren't growing spiritually. They read all the latest self-help books and blogs about the journey to a happier you, but are neglecting the fact that they need to dig a little deeper and seek the Lord for wisdom and understanding. There is a plethora of amazing information available, but if our foundation isn't a relationship with the Lord and His word, we leave ourselves as an open target. It's easy to be so full of pride and the lies from the enemy that we begin to believe what the enemy says. He plants a seed of inadequacy and we begin to question it, asking ourselves, "Could this be true?"

When you have a relationship with God and you are in His word, as soon as the enemy tries to bother you, immediately reply, "Greater is He that is in me than He that is in the world." When we are guarded with the truth, lies have no foundation. There is no possible way you will get to your purpose without a fight. The enemy knows what is in store for you and will do anything to distract you, delay you, or stop you from getting to your greater. The enemy will never be able to fight the promise that is in God's hand, but he will definitely fight your obedience.

People question that if God is so great, loving and powerful, why do His people have to endure pain and trials. The answer is simple: so that we remain humble and continually magnify God, not ourselves. Humans are forgetful. We tend to have selective memory and to behave like the Chief Cupbearer that Joseph encountered, who forgot to mention to Pharaoh how Joseph helped him. We get so wrapped up in ourselves that we forget what God has done, but it's hard to forget pain. Painful situations help us grow. When you remember the pain, you will remember how God delivered you from that pain and that you are healed and whole.

There is a reason for every season. Everything that you have endured is for a greater purpose. Trust the process, and most of all, trust the Lord.

LESSON #2:

Get Ready to Fight.

"Arise, for it is your task, and we are with you, be strong and do it." Ezra 10:4

No matter how you feel, if God says, "Do it," you have to. It can be difficult to decipher if you are being led by the Lord or your feelings and own will. Whenever there is peace, you are in the flow of the Holy Spirit. "For God is not a God of confusion but of peace" 1 Corinthians 14:33. Whenever there is chaos and confusion, heed to the spirit and ask the Lord to lead you to whatever needs to be done. Be mindful that when we pray bold prayers, we must be willing to follow what comes after. I remember praying, "God if this relationship is not of you, show me, make it clear, and remove me from this situation."

Every time I prayed that prayer, the person and I would argue, and it was horrible. But I wasn't ready to step out in faith and follow God, so I prayed that prayer a few times. The final time I uttered the words was when I knew, without a doubt, that I had to obey the Lord and end it. That is when I realized my purpose meant more than my comfort. My purpose means more than my feelings and my fear of being alone. I decided to activate my faith and truly believe that God will be with me. The entire body of Christ is waiting for you to get into position. Stop telling God all the reasons why you think you cannot do what He is asking. Read His word to confirm why He has chosen you and why you have to complete the task. We all have a purpose that is given by God, so why do we try to accomplish it in our own will? We have to focus on the Lord. Psalm 57:2 reads "I cry out to God most high, to God who fulfills his purpose for me." Note that the verse says "His purpose," not "my" purpose. We have to live our lives in ways that glorify God. Jesus stood naked on a cross for you, and was spit on and beaten because He loves you. If you are reading this and you feel the Holy Spirit tugging at your heart, say this prayer:

Father, help me. Strengthen me where I am weak and help me to continue moving forward. Show me the things I need to remove and the people I need to love from a distance. Change my heart, Lord. Remove the things in me that are not of you right now. Guide me. Draw closer to me, Lord. I want to be closer to you. I want to live a life that is pleasing to you. Wreck me, Lord. Wreck the plans that I had for my life and write your plans, Lord. I submit my life to you.

In Jesus' mighty name, Amen.

You have a pulse, which means you still have purpose. If you are unsure about what that purpose may be, go before the Lord and ask Him. Ask your pastor to help you interpret what you believe God is saying to you. There will be times when you feel confused or when you are not sure you should continue. That is perfectly fine. In due season, everything will align. Hold on to the promises of God. Pray that God surrounds you with people who will help you on the journey of fulfilling your God given purpose. Embrace the season of preparation. When God hides you and strips you of distractions, take that time to truly fall in love with Jesus and with yourself.

Be mindful not to share your dream with everyone. Use discretion when identifying people to assist you, and with whom you can confide. Be aware of those who will try to attach themselves to your blessing. There is a huge difference between those who are assigned and those who are attached.

LESSON #3:

Do Not Abort the Process.

"Therefore do not throw away your confidence, which has a great reward. For you have need of endurance, so that when you have done the will of God you may receive what is promised, For, 'Yet a little while, and the coming one will come and will not delay; but my righteous one shall live by faith, and if he shrinks back, my soul has no pleasure in him.' But we are not of those who shrink back and are destroyed, but of those who have faith and preserve their souls." Hebrews 10: 35-39

We must fight the good fight of faith. Faith is far from easy but without it we are purposeless. Without obedience, what is the point? Don't settle for a mediocre life that society is trying to sell you, press through focused on the Lord and go after the life He created you for. Read Hebrews 10:19-39, 11, and 12, and get excited about your life! No matter where you have been, remember if you have a pulse you have a purpose. GO BE GREAT!

CLOSING PRAYER

Dear Lord,

I pray right now for the person that read this book, who desires to hear from you. I pray for wisdom, courage, discernment, strength, perseverance, and most of all faith in you, Lord. Let my brother- or sister-in-Christ genuinely seek you.

I pray that a fire is ignited inside of them that no man or devil will be able to put out. I pray that you create in them a clean heart, renew their minds, and pour fresh oil upon them, Father. We want to know our purpose so we can diligently serve you and your kingdom.

Help us be more like you and less like this fallen world. Change us, mold us, and shape us to be like you. Grant us peace and allow the confusion to cease. Speak to us, Lord; we are ready to abide in you.

In Jesus' precious and holy name.

AMEN.

ABOUT ASHLEY PORTER

There's no escaping the calling over your life. No one knows that better than **Ashley Porter** who not only embraces her divine purpose, but helps others do the same.

Through blogging, motivational speaking and volunteering, Ashley is committed to breaking generational curses and reclaiming family unity. This dedication affirmed her decision to enroll in Lancaster Bible College where she's studying Biblical Studies.

She is also the founder of Goal Getters Empowerment Association, which encourages youth and young adults to build positive self-image and the confidence needed to achieve their greatest goals and potential. Ashley is faith-fueled and purpose-driven with Christ at the center of her life. In spite of life's obstacles, she stands firm on the words of Philippians 4:13.

Ashley is a resident of Columbia, Maryland, and enjoys traveling, loving and laughing with her son, Daniel. She's a multi-talented soul, skilled at writing, event planning, arts and crafts, modeling and ripping the runway. Get to know more about Ashley by visiting her online at www.GoalGettersEmpowerment.com.

WE WANT TO HEAR FROM YOU!!!

If this book has made a difference in your life
Ashley would be delighted to hear about it.

Leave a review on Amazon.com!

BOOK ASHLEY TO SPEAK AT YOUR NEXT EVENT!

Send an email to booking@publishyourgift.com

Learn more about Ashley at
www.GoalGettersEmpowerment.com

FOLLOW ASHLEY ON SOCIAL MEDIA

  @Ashley_Speaks_

 /GoalGelttersEmpowerment

"EMPOWERING YOU TO IMPACT GENERATIONS"
WWW.PUBLISHYOURGIFT.COM

CPSIA information can be obtained
at www.ICGtesting.com
Printed in the USA
FFOW01n0212100615
14149FF